Siberian Husky

The Ultimate Pet Guide for Siberian Husky

Siberian Husky General Info, Purchasing, Care, Cost, Keeping, Health, Supplies, Food, Breeding and More Included!

By Lolly Brown

Foreword

If you plan in owning a Siberian Husky as a pet, you might as well put a tag on him saying "I'm not a wolf." Don't be surprise if people you run into the streets will ask you if you're keeping a wolf because if you put a Siberian Husky dog beside an actual wolf you won't be able to see which is which. It takes a special keeper to raise a Siberian Husky as this dog breed is strong and full of energy. Siberian husky like most dogs is very loyal to their keepers. They sometimes come across as quite sappy and mature but they are very playful pets that love to hang out with people and other dog breeds.

As cool and awesome as they may sound, keeping Siberian huskies as pets is not for everyone. It takes someone as brave and strong as this breed is, and it's definitely not meant to be kept as a "normal" household pet especially if you have very young children. They are friendly creatures looking for a home just like any other dog breeds; they need someone responsible and free –spirited yet mature to match their personality. The question is – do you have what it takes to become a Siberian Husky keeper? See if you can be part of the pack by learning how to take care of this dog breed. You'll learn everything you need to know in becoming a responsible dog keeper to your Siberian Husky in this guidebook.

Table of Contents

Introduction

If you're the kind of person who loves the outdoors and do activities like camping, trekking and hiking, then you'll definitely enjoy hanging out with this wolf lookalike. Siberian huskies don't mind carrying a light load, travelling up a hill or mountain, and experience some form of physical challenge. They love adventure and want to be where the action is. This dog breed is very athletic, smart, active, and tough. Literally and figuratively speaking, they can weather the storm.

Siberian Huskies like wolves are animal breed who likes to be in a pack. They would prefer being raised around people and also having company around them. This dog breed can find escape routes if you're not always there to keep them company; this is their natural instinct. As a potential keeper you need to be as smart, agile, and alert as your Siberian husky.

Siberian huskies may look intimidating and scary at first, and they will pretty much give you that wolfish aura the first time you meet them but they are gentle creatures that can cozy up even with kids as long as you supervise them. Many people expect them to act as tough guard dogs but they're not, though of course they serve as protectors and a loyal companion to their keepers especially if they or their owners are being threatened.

If you're looking for a dog breed who likes to play around the house, you can count on the Siberian husky to give you a bit of entertainment through their antics; they love playing with toys and with themselves which can definitely amuse the whole family. However don't let this breed's playfulness fool you because unlike most house dogs, the Siberian Husky isn't a people pleaser. Sometimes they have a mind of their own and won't follow whatever you bid them to do which is why it can be quite challenging in keeping this dog breed as pets especially if you haven't had any experience owning a dog before.

Don't be put off by people who will tell you that it isn't possible to train a Siberian husky, find out if you have what it takes to become a keeper of this wolf lookalike. It all depends on the choices you make for your pet and the patience you show. If you are lucky enough to be a Siberian Husky owner, then congratulations! You're in for a treat!

This guidebook will provide you with information about the dog's history, breed standard, temperament and behavior as well as the basic things you need to know like how to keep a Siberian Husky healthy, the right diet, grooming and training techniques as well as the requirements needed for them to feel at home in your place.

Chapter One: Origin and History

Siberian Huskies originated from the cold land of Siberia. It was discovered by a tribe known as the Chukchi who lived along the cold Arctic coast of the northeastern side of the country, where they hunted for seal and battled the severe weather. The Chukchi tribe needed a companion that's strong enough to help them in hauling their harvests as they mostly carry loads of seals that came from Anadyr River. They develop a dog breed that can be used as a working dog, can withstand against the harsh weather, and also friendly to people. This was how the breed was developed some 3000 years ago. In this chapter, you'll get to learn more about the history of Siberian Huskies, their origins, and some general information you need to know as potential pet keepers.

A Brief History of Siberian Huskies

The gentleness of Siberian huskies is mostly because these dogs lived around people for a long time, and were tasked to pull sleds, and carry heavy loads. They only became aggressive if they were let loose by their keepers to satisfy their hunting instincts. The Chukchi dog became so much part of the tribe that it even became a status symbol. In fact, back then the wealth of a Chukchi man was measured by the number and quality of his Siberian huskies. This dog also became part of folklores and religious beliefs.

Around the 19th century, when the Chukchi tribe managed to temporarily escape the Czar's troops, Siberian huskies became quite important and significant especially when the fur trade opened up. Even if the Chukchi tribe became under siege, they somewhat managed to survive, all thanks to the Siberian husky pack as they were faster than reindeers when it comes to pulling the sleds. In 1908, fur traders from Alaska came home with some of these Chukchi dogs, and they were renamed as Siberian Husky.

Today, these dogs are still used for dogsled racing, and they're still much faster than other sled dog breeds like the Alaskan Malamute and Samoyed breed. The dog breed is also quite popular when it comes to a European sport called Skijoring and Ski – Pulka where dogs pulls a skier to win the race. The Siberian Husky has also been recognized by several dog organizations around the world including the American Kennel Club and British Kennel Club.

And because the Siberian huskies are gentle, they became popular household pets despite of their wild and hunting nature. They can go along with people and kids as long as there's adult supervision and they also love hanging out with other dog breeds. However, they may not be advisable if you have other pets like cats, birds, rabbits, chickens, reptiles, and the likes because they still have that predator instinct in them. They can ultimately see your smaller pets as prey and not as friends. Today, most keepers use Siberian huskies as a dog companion in trekking and backpacking adventures.

Siberian Husky as Pets

As pets these dogs are not high maintenance, they only require a simple diet, low – cost housing requirements, and also minimal grooming. They do shed quite a lot and may need a good brushing but they have no 'doggy' smell and are pretty hygienic. They also do not need frequent baths. General speaking, Siberian Huskies are healthy dogs that can live for 11 to 15 years on average, and they only face health issues when they grow old.

What they need though is a lot of activity and exercise. You need to ensure that you keep them busy otherwise they might find a way to escape and satisfy their thirst for adventure. So better prepare trips here and there, and take them out on walks or better yet let them do some forms of work like helping you carry around construction materials or whatnot.

Siberian Husky General Characteristics

Despite the wolfish looks, these dogs do not have any biological link with wolves. They are purebred domestic dogs that possess a powerful appearance. Siberian huskies have double coats that are mostly colored black and white, copper red and white, or gray and white. Some huskies possess pure white or even brown, reddish and biscuit shading coats. These dogs also have very unique facial patterns or markings; have white feet and legs as well as tail tips that add to its wolfish look. They possess a light blue eyes though some have one blue eye and the other is a hazel or brown color.

Since Siberian Huskies are working dogs you can pretty much expect them to really pull heavy loads. It is a medium-sized dog that weighs an average of 35 to 60 pounds with an average height of 51 - 60 cm. They might be medium in size but they are sometimes much stronger than large sized dogs.

Siberian huskies are truly one of a kind because they possess that balance of beauty and endurance. They are pretty straightforward pets, easy to live with, easy to care for, easy to get along with, and also a loyal and energetic house companion. They love to roam around, and can also be trained. The Siberian Huskies have come a long way from being working dogs as they now have become part of an elite breed of pets that define their keeper as someone who should be intelligent, mature, adventurous and have a wolf – like characteristic just like them – by that I mean loyal and knows how to work with a group. As a potential keeper you need to provide them with affection, attention, training, friendship and most importantly love and respect. If you do that, they'll also do the same for you, and it will be one great experience!

Chapter Two: Personality of the Siberian Husky

Aside from their amazing wolfish appearance, the personality of the Siberian Husky is what strikes most dog enthusiasts. It seems that their intimidating wolfish looks are just a front for their friendly, loving, gentle and smart characteristic. They make great companion dogs if they are loved, respected and trained with patience. A lot of people feel that they are predator dogs with wolf blood in them but nothing can be farther from the truth. This chapter will shed light on what you can expect when keeping Siberian huskies as pets. Find out if this dog breed is right for you by checking if their personality somewhat matches yours or better yet complement your own characteristic as a keeper.

Temperament and Behavior of Siberian Huskies

Even if they are a gentle breed to humans and other dogs, Siberian huskies are still predators when it comes to other animals especially smaller breeds. Their killer instincts are awakened if they see pets like birds, cats, rabbits, guinea pigs, lizards, turtles, and the likes. After all they were raised as working dogs who hunted to fend for themselves in the summer seasons back in the day. They are a devoted companion for the Chukchi tribe which is why they became very friendly to people but not to pets. Even if you trained them or do a proper pet introduction, it's not advisable that you left them alone with your other pets because their predator instincts can kicked in.

Below are some of the personalities that make up a Siberian Husky:

The Friendly Dog

Siberian huskies are sweet and love to socialize with other people. As a matter of fact, they are quite lousy guard dogs because they can also become friendly with strangers. Essentially, these dog breed is a friendly creatures that simply loves meeting people. Siberian huskies are fearless and most of the time unsuspicious of humans, since the breed has been raised around them. They know that humans are their friends and prefer their companionship. And since they love being with the pack like the wolves, they hate being alone so ensure that you keep them company or leave them with another dog if you're not around.

They seek constant interaction and don't like being left alone in an apartment. They would want to go outside, roam the area, dig around, and be where you are or where other people are. Even if they are active breeds, they can sit and watch with your family because they simply like the idea of 'togetherness.' You cannot find another breed as friendly as the Siberian Husky because they really value your friendship.

The Loving Buddy

They're not the usual lap dogs but they are capable of a lot of love. They protect their owners like how parents protect their kids; they'll do what they can, not just for their keeper but their keeper's family. In fact, many owners have trained their huskies to be protective of their children because this breed loves children. There is a special bond between these dog breed and children, and it's probably because the women of the Chukchi tribe back in the day raised the husky pups and their own children together.

You can expect your Siberian husky to be gentle, protective, and affectionate to your kids but it's still best that you keep an eye out and supervise your dog especially if you have very young children to avoid any mishaps. After all, they're still animals.

Siberian huskies are a loving dog breed that may not be very expressive of his love but shows it in other ways like being protective and friendly. The Siberian husky will show you how protective he is but will not display any possessiveness about you. This breed knows how to keep a distance and respects a person's space. He has a loving soul that will transcend in you when you spend time with them.

The Playful Pet

Like most dogs, Siberian huskies are very playful and have a sense of humor. There's nothing that this breed enjoys more than a playful fight with you on the carpet or the on the ground. He loves playing with kids and toys. It's highly recommended that you provide him with his own toys too. You'll definitely have a good laugh at their silly antics, and amusing tricks.

If you're looking to play fetch with him, it may not be the right one for you because that's something that they're not fond of, although they can of course be trained but don't expect them to do it like what a retriever dog breed does. Running is a natural instinct for this dog breed, and it's also a way for them to express their free spirited personality.

You can take them out with you if you're biking or jogging around. One of the downside to this playful personality is that it can him to wander off which is why they should always be on the leash especially if you're going to take them out for a walk, they shouldn't be left to their own devises as they can get easily distracted by people and other things.

The Smart Husky

Siberian huskies are highly intelligent creatures that don't need to get told what to do. They have that uncanny ability to know just what is needed from him. You will find that your Siberian husky will be very reserved, docile, and disciplined inside the house so you don't have to worry about them bumping into your stuff and messing up your house. They need the respect but they also need to be intelligently shown who the boss is.

Siberian huskies are intelligent enough to get away with punishments and any negative reinforcements which mean that you'll need to deal with this mature dog in a very mature way. The personality of the Siberian husky is similar to that of the wolves, where they follow orders from the "alpha dog" of the pack. You need to show him that you're the alpha dog.

The Stubborn Attitude

Though not totally stubborn, Siberian huskies still show that stubborn side in them from time to time. It's probably because they are mature and clever dogs that are also confident in their own skin.

A Siberian husky may not listen to you simply because he doesn't want to or because you didn't ask respectfully! They know what they deserve! You can circumvent this stubborn attitude by simply being the more matured and smart keeper that acts as the leader or the alpha dog. Once they know who is in charge, their stubborn attitude will not be a problem. You need to exercise patience and firmness especially when you're training them.

The Energetic Animal

Since Siberian huskies are energetic and active pets, you can expect them to always have an alert mind, and lively attitude. They are quite optimistic and confident creatures. They also possess a fearless personality since their breed was raised in extreme conditions. Sometimes being smart and active can arouse curiosity. They are inquisitive of their current surroundings and will definitely check everything out in your house or in your neighbor's backyard just to see it for themselves.

You don't want them getting bored as it could mean trouble. If they are bored, you can find them digging up the ground and chewing stuff. He can also mess up the plants, lawns, and even your bed! So better keep them busy and satisfy their curious minds.

Hunter or Home Buddy?

The Siberian husky may look wild and a creature that'll bite you but it's not. In fact, this breed is more a companion dog than hunter. It isn't a big dog but is very powerful and the strength shows in his body. The persona of the huskies is quite in contrast with its appearance and origins

As a working dog that hunted in the wild and originally a working pet, the Siberian husky has the personality of a happy home buddy. These breed will always pick being a good companion than being a hunter like wolves. It can still be quite challenging for first time dog keepers but as long as you provide them with adequate attention and training, you'll soon find out that they're hunting side is just one of their special skills, and not a personality.

Pros and Cons of Keeping Siberian Huskies

Pros:

- Friendly to adults, seniors, children, and even strangers
- Playful and active
- Loyal and protective of its owners
- Highly trainable
- Tolerant
- Gets along with other dog breeds
- Smart and curious
- Reserved and calm
- Has a wolfish appearance and docile demeanor around the house

Cons:

- Sometimes curiosity leads to stubbornness
- Can get easily bored and if it does can result to chewing stuff
- Can sometimes resist commands given to them
- Can be aggressive towards smaller animals like cats
- Can be quite high maintenance in terms of food and housing needs
- Demands exercise, attention, and training

Chapter Three: Is Siberian Husky the Right Breed for You?

Perhaps the better question is this: Are you the right keeper for the Siberian Husky? As mentioned earlier, it takes a special person to be the owner of this awesome breed, and if you are thinking of bringing him home you must be sure of why you want him as a pet. Siberian huskies are not the kind of breed suitable for first time dog keepers, and even if you have previously owned a dog breed before like Shi Tzus, Teacup Yorkies, or a Golden Retriever you'll surely see how different it is in keeping such a breed like the Siberian Husky.

For you to successfully care for a Siberian husky, you would need to have previous experience with handling dog breeds as big and as clever as they are. You'll need to train them well enough and give them a kind of tough love so to speak. They're not lap dogs though they enjoy affection; they're quite independent dogs that are in need of independent and confident owners.

Don't be fooled by their Appearance

The reason why many Siberian husky ends up in adoption centers is because most keepers only bought it because they look fearless. Sure, physical appearance is one of the factors of why people get a dog in the first place but as what Siberian huskies have proven over and over again – looks aren't everything. There are many Siberian Huskies that have been abandoned because their keepers brought them home thinking their attractively fearless look would make them great guard dogs but as you now know this dog breed will welcome any strangers with open arms so to speak. They are very gentle to all types of people – and that includes burglars which makes them lousy guard dogs.

Sometimes these pets get abandoned because their owners became overwhelmed with their constant shedding. This breed has a double coat so don't be surprised there's a lot of shedding. At first look, their coat is not too long but the undercoat can be quite especially during summertime; you can also see some bald patches from time to time.

How to determine if this is the right breed for you?

This section will provide you with some things you need to consider before acquiring a Siberian husky as house pet. The best way to answer this question is to examine your own expectations of what you are seeking from this dog breed that you can't seem to find in other dogs. What's your purpose? Are you part of the professional breeder looking to join this dog breed for show? Do you have children? Are you and your family looking for a household pet? Are you a single person in search of a friendly buddy? Do you love training dogs and playing with them? Are you adventurous or do you like to go on trips? These are just some of the questions you need to ponder on. Below are some things that can help you determine if the Siberian husky is the right breed for you:

Are you a first time dog owner or experienced keeper?

If you have had another dog breed as a pet, you should know that all dog breeds have different characteristics. As for the Siberian husky, this dog breed is a confident, independent pack dog that has a mind of its own which is why training can be quite a challenge even for experienced dog keepers. You will need to prove your dominance (like the alpha dog in a pack) which is why some amount of keeping experience can be helpful.

Chapter Three: Is Siberian Husky The Right Breed For You?

Do you live in a house or an apartment?

Since Siberian huskies are quite large dogs that like to stay outdoors, you need to ensure that he can have more than enough space to roam around with even if you live in an apartment, you should be able to provide him with adequate exercise. If you live in a one – room apartment, you may need to get a bigger place, either that or give up keeping this dog. On the other hand if you live in a house then ensure that you put up a secure fence in your backyard or garden to prevent your pet from escaping. This is because the Siberian Husky's curiosity will eventually lead him in finding escape routes. If you live on a farm, it's important that you always keep an eye out because there'll be too much temptation around him by hunting down smaller animals like rabbits, chickens, birds, and the likes.

What are the weather conditions or seasons in your place of residence?

Siberian huskies are originally from the cold land of Siberia, they developed double coats and dense furs because they were born and raised in cold conditions but you can still keep them even if you live in humid places like Florida or Los Angeles. During the summer season you will just have to make sure that have access to water and also a shade; provide them with a bit of air-conditioning if possible. It's better if you get a Siberian Husky from your local area so that the dog is already accustomed to the weather and wouldn't have a hard time adjusting.

Are you looking for a household family pet?

Despite their wolfish and fearless look, this breed is one of the best dog breeds that are perfect family pets. Unlike most dog breeds, Siberian huskies love everyone in the family! They tend to be close to not just one member but also to the whole family. They love to play games, make a family laugh, and are also tolerant of human behavior. On the other hand if you're looking to just get a dog and let him stay outside and not have any sort of interaction, then the Siberian husky is not for the breed for you. They can be trained to live in kennels but this is a breed that is happiest when they are inside the house with their owners.

Do you want a dog that will be gentle to your kids or a breed that will protect your children?

Siberian huskies as mentioned earlier are very gentle, protective, and love to play with children which are why they are perfect family pets. You can be sure that your kids are safe with them though it's still best that you supervise them especially for very young children as they might get excited and want to play with a toddler and knock him or her down in the process. Siberian Huskies will love to engage in a lot of activity with the children and will never intentionally bite or harm a child. This dog breed is protective of children in the sense that if a stranger came into the house, they would put themselves ahead of the child to protect him/ her.

Do you want a Siberian husky for security purposes?

If you're someone looking to acquire a Siberian husky as a watchdog, then better forget this breed because this kind of dog don't have any sense of ownership which means they are not mean to strangers. The Siberian husky is also not a barker. If ever he does bark it's not because there's an intruder in your house, it's usually because they are sad and alone. If you're looking to get Siberian husky to watch over your house or property when you're not around, well it's not going to work as this breed tends to easily trust human beings and wouldn't be able to tell if a person has good or bad intentions.

Do you work at home or do you have a 9 to 5 job?

If you're a freelancer or someone who works alone at the comfort of your home, then it's wise to get a Siberian husky to keep you company. On the other hand, if you are planning to locked up your husky while you're off to your 9 to 5 job then it's best to not keep this dog as a pet because they don't like being left alone. If you do this, they'll most likely get bored and end up messing your apartment/ house. They'll also howl loudly which can be a problem for your other neighbors. If you always leave him alone, they'll eventually find a way to break out of the house and wander off. Always remember that this dog is meant to socialize with people or at least with its keeper.

Are you a neat freak or always want things to be organized?

If you are, then getting this breed is not ideal. First off, Siberian huskies will tend to shed a lot, leaving locks of coats around the house. They might also mess up your house every now and then especially if they're bored. If you have a garden, this dog will definitely dig up your lawn, run around your flowers or vegetables, and even hop over the fence. This is the reason why you'll need to have a fence strong and high enough to keep your pet from finding escape routes. If the dog you'll get is a digger, then it's best that you provide a sand box for him/ her to keep him occupied.

Do you want an obedient dog or a breed you can walk around without it's leashed on?

Siberian huskies can be trained and can follow orders from their keepers, but they're not like retriever dog breeds that will always follow every command. As mentioned earlier, they have this clever and independent characteristic which makes them relatively obedient but not entirely a follower. This dog breed is also born to run which is why a Siberian Husky must always be on the leash when you are walking him or running with him. They will not listen to you once they set off on a chase and they could get lost because they are not capable of finding their way back home.

Do you have other household pets?

Housing a Siberian Husky with other pets like cats, birds, and rabbits or other smaller creatures is a big NO – NO. It doesn't matter if you trained or do a proper pet introduction because Siberian huskies still have that hunting instinct in them that could trigger if smaller pets other than dog breeds are around the house. Do not expect a Siberian Husky to be nice to other animals as well. This also applies for dogs that are still small. If your other pet is also a Siberian Husky, then the two dogs will get along very well as they are part of a pack and that makes them happy with you as the alpha dog or the leader. Expect them to always play and wrestle with each other.

Can you provide enough time and attention to these pets?

Siberian huskies are generally easy to care for but they do need lots of exercise, grooming, and fun time with the family. They are very easy going in the sense that they will not need constant attention from you but you need to be around to make them happy and not succumb to loneliness or boredom.

The Siberian Husky is not for you if:

- If you are a first time dog keeper
- If you prefer to have a watchdog or guard dog to look over your property and kids
- If you are out of the house most of the time because of work
- If you don't have the time to supervise the dog
- If you are looking for a pet that always want to cuddle and show affection to you
- If you want a lap dog
- If you want to get a dog that will follow every order you give him or play catch with.
- If you want a dog breed that can go off without being leashed

- If you keep other smaller animals
- If you are allergic to dog fur as this breed sheds a lot
- If you like everything to be organized and neat especially in your garden
- If you don't like an active dog

The Siberian Husky is suited for you if:

- If you previously owned other dog breeds
- If you want a dog that will get along with the family
- If you want to have a dog that'll be gentle to your kids
- If you have a yard and garden that's secured and properly fenced
- If you like a low maintenance dog
- If you want a hygienic dog that's odor free
- If you prefer a mature and reserved dog breed
- If you can tolerate excessive shedding
- If you can commit to give time to walk him around and provide adequate amount of exercise
- If you are firm and patient especially when it comes to training
- If you're not going to leave him alone all the time and if you have enough time to interact with him.

Chapter Four: Choosing a Siberian Husky and a Reputable Breeder

Assuming you have decided to get a Siberian husky as a pet, the next step is to find out where you can get a dog that is of good quality. The breed's increasing popularity has made it available in pet shops, online pet stores, private breeders, and also backyard breeders. When it comes to finding the right Siberian husky for you, you need to make sure that you're going to get it from someone responsible and reputable. You can contact your local dog club for a list of recommended breeders near your area or you can also refer to the Siberian Husky Club of America website for a breeder referral directory. This chapter will provide you with a checklist in finding the right breeder and quality dog.

Siberian Husky Club of America Guidelines in Finding a Reputable Breeder

The SHCA does have guidelines for breeders who are in the business of breeding the Siberian Husky to improve and maintain the pedigree, rather than for the money. Here are some things to keep in mind when selecting the right breeder:

- The breeder joins or takes part in Siberian Husky activities and/ or competitions.

- The breeder should explain both the pros and cons of keeping a Siberian Husky

- The breeder shouldn't attempt to sell you a pup that's less than 8 weeks since this is a crucial period for newborns to still be with their mothers.

- The breeder should want to ensure that their pets will go to caring families and good homes. If the breeder is asking you questions about where you live, if you have children who will not be abusive, your working hours, and financial status etc. This will show that they are concerned that their dogs get a caring family.

- The breeder should give detailed guidelines of what is required to raise a Siberian Husky.

- The breeder should be able to provide you with the dog's health and breeding history like the dates and types of vaccinations/ worming / other medical procedures given as well as feeding instructions and registration papers if any.

- The breeder should give you a fixed time period within which you can take the pup to visit a vet.

- The breeder should show his support and help to other Siberian husky breeders and show dogs.

- The breeder should have contacts with rescue organizations as this will show that he/she really cares for this breed.

- The breeder should know the current genetic research of the breed because it will show you that he/she is update, and knows how to eliminate any possible hereditary defects.

- The breeder should be able to make a thorough analysis and evaluation of a sire and a dam (male / female dogs respectively) to ensure that they are healthy for breeding.

- The breeder shouldn't breed dogs that are not 2 years and above

- The breeder shouldn't be involved in any deal with pet shop or wholesalers if he/she claims to be a private breeder.

- The breeder should show his/ her concerns regarding protecting the breeding standards for Siberian huskies and dogs in general.

Evaluating a Reputable Breeder

Below are some of the questions you should you're your prospective breeder especially if you'll have the chance to tour around their breeding facilities:

- Where are the parents of the pups? Ask if you can see them to ensure that they are healthy. A healthy parent means a healthy offspring.

- Can I see medical records if the parents have been screened for canine hip dysplasia and eye disease? This is a common illness and genetic defect among Siberian huskies.

- What are the ways you've tried in improving the breed?

- How do you socialize your pups?

- Are there any tests you have recently done? What and when the pups did receive vaccinations?

- Do you join kennel or dog shows? Why?

- Do you have contact numbers of dog organizations or rescue centers?

- Can you provide reference numbers from other breeders or customers who know you?

Chapter Four: Choosing a Siberian Husky & Reputable Breeder

Frequently Asked Questions

Can I acquire a Siberian Husky from adoption centers or rescue centers?

If you're going to acquire a Siberian husky from adoption centers, it would be wise to do careful and thorough medical check – up before committing to adopt a certain breed. Usually pets that are abandoned don't have any illness or whatnot; it's just that their owners could not cope up with the requirements of keeping one. Most Siberian huskies end up in shelters because of incompetent handling of their keepers. If there's no problem in its health, and if the dog exhibits good temperament, and is well – mannered then by all means adopt it or rescue it from the shelter.

Should I choose a spayed/ neutered dog?

The answer to this highly depends if you wanted to eventually transition from being a simple keeper to a dog breeder. However, not everyone can breed a Siberian husky, you need to take the time to learn about how you can successfully breed a healthy litter not to mention be knowledgeable about the dog's genetic composition. This is why a good breeder will insist that you take home a spayed or a neutered Siberian Husky. If you are a professional who owns a show Siberian or a racer/sledding Siberian, then you might retain co-breeding rights with the breeder and have a detailed contract written out. However if it is pet quality Siberian Husky you want, it is much wiser to choose a spayed or a neutered one.

How much does this breed costs?

Pet quality Siberian Husky puppies cost anywhere between $500 to $600. If you're opting for a show quality pet you can expect the price to reach $1000 or even more. Some pet shops and backyard breeders will sell it for a bargain of around $200 to $400 but be careful because most of the time the breeds coming from such sources are from puppy mills, and there's a huge chance that these dogs are ill or aggressive since they're not properly raised and cared for unlike if you're acquiring from a reputable private breeder.

Tips in Selecting the Right Siberian Husky Pup

- The pup should be active, alert, and sociable

- The pup shouldn't be afraid of other puppies or humans

- The pup should have no eyes and ears discharge and shouldn't be pot – bellied.

- The gums should be pink in color.

- The pup shouldn't resist whenever you hold them or aren't afraid of human interaction, this is a sign that they have been properly socialized.

- The pups should have the right weight for its age.

- The pup's coat should be free of fleas, dirt and bald patches

- They shouldn't have diarrhea or should have a clean bottom.

Tips in Selecting the Right Siberian Husky Adult

- The dog should already be house broken which means that he/she should know basic commands, and have already formed good behavior patterns.

- If you're acquiring a pet from rescue centers, it's wise to find out why they were abandoned in the first place.

- It's ideal to find out what the dog's habits is, its temperament, how he/ she respond to commands, daily routine and also its history.

- Check their overall health status

- The dog should be alert, has a pleasant disposition and quite mischievous

- The body is free of any discharge, patches, and the fur should be clean and well – groomed.

- The husky shouldn't be fat or bulky; it should be a moderate sized dog with a compact body.

- The husky should be balanced whenever he stands or moves

- The husky shouldn't have any mobility problems; he should be light on his feet if he walks

- The husky should show elegance, speed, and power

- The dog shouldn't be taller than 23 ½ inches for a male and no taller than 22 inches for females.

Chapter Five: Housing Needs and Requirements of Siberian Huskies

Once you have finally acquired your newfound pet, it's time to prepare your home and have that warm welcome so that your Siberian Husky can immediately the love from you and your family. As mentioned before, your house should not be cramped and should have more than enough space to accommodate your Siberian Husky. Make sure that your pet will have room to move around safely and freely. Among the things you need to do is acquire the dog items that your pet will need. Don't worry because this chapter will have a list of the things you need to buy for dog keeping.

It's also important that before your pet arrives, you and your family have thought about the rules inside the house for your new pet. This section will help you get started, read on!

Things to do Before Bringing Your Pet Home

Task#1: Choose your dog's veterinarian. Choosing a vet for your new dog is the first step especially during the period where the breeder is still finalizing the process of giving you your prospective Siberian Husky. It will enable you to have your vet thoroughly check the dog's health, and you can also get advice on what you would need in terms of nutrition, the emergency medicines, and advice on how to make him comfortable in your house.

Task#2: Learn, learn, learn! After you've read this basic manual, it's wise to just keep learning and educating yourself about how to successfully keep a Siberian husky. Get information from other breeders, from several online resources, and from pet owners. You can also opt to join dog clubs or attend dog competitions. Take the time to talk to them, discuss it with your family, and also be mentally prepared for change around the house to enjoy the benefits of a pet like the Siberian Husky.

Task#3: Buy everything your Siberian Husky needs. You can get advice from your breeder about the things that your new pet will need before he/she arrives. Your breeder's task is to guide you on where to buy stuff, how much is needed, suggested brands etc. Some of these essential things include the following:

- Food and Water bowls
- Dog crate and bed
- Chew sticks
- Leash and collar
- Dog friendly shampoo and conditioner; toothbrush and toothpaste
- Steel comb (wide – toothed)
- Flea comb/ Bristle brush
- Towel
- Mat
- Medicines, first – aid kit
- Dog tags
- Quality food/ puppy treats
- Gates and latches for pups
- Toys
- Nail clippers/ grooming scissors
-

Task#4: Decide on where the potty spot will be located. Before your pet even arrives, you need to be able to set up the cage already, and most importantly decide on where they will relieve themselves. Potty training is one of the first things you want to do as it will save you a lot of headaches in the onset. The potty spot is the same spot where your dog would be brought back to again and again. Begin to familiarize your Siberian husky from Day 1, and before you take him inside the house. Also decide on the times you and other members of the family take the pet out. For a puppy it would be every three hours and after every meal.

Task#5: Schedule feeding time. You and your family should take turns when feeding your Siberian husky so that your dog will recognize that he is really part of the pack. Most husky puppies will eat 4 times a day at least until they reach 18 months, once they hit adulthood, they'll normally just eat twice a day. Feed your Husky at the same times every day and in the same place. You should make it a point to take them out to the potty spot after their food.

Task#6: Puppy – proof your house. Before your pet arrives, take the time to check if there's anything that will be unsafe for your pet – because there'll be a lot. Keep in mind that Siberian huskies are smart and always curious. Get him out of danger by following some tips below:

- Electric cords and electronic gadgets should be out of sight or out of reach
- Always keep the trashcan covered so as not to make your pet curious about it.
- If you have screens, ensure that there are no wires or strings sticking out that could harm them.

- o Always close the bathroom doors and don't left them unsupervised to the rooms you don't want to get messed up.
- o Shoes and clothes should always be in the closet and out of reach as they may chew it
- o Make sure that the medicines and other chemicals as well as kitchen stuff are also out of reach.

Task#7: Tight security is a must. Siberian huskies will always find a way to escape the house not because they don't want to live with you but because they're just really curious of what's out there in the world. This is why you must seal all possible escape routes and fenced him in securely. Ensure that you check for loose gates, easily un - lockable doors and windows if you live an apartment. If you have a backyard or garden, make sure that you secure any escape routes. Siberian huskies especially when they reached their full size can easily jump over a low fence or dig under it which is why you will likely need a 5 to 6 foot fence, gate or sturdy blockage. You will have to ensure that there are no gaps and prevent him from building a tunnel – because they can! It's also wise to not place any chairs, tables, benches, and other flat surfaces where your pet can climb on and use as paddle board to jump over the fence.

Task#8: Remove any toxic objects. If you have a garden, there could be some plants and flowers that can be toxic for your pet, which is why you should take the time to know what, can be poisonous for your pet so that you can remove it before he comes in. If you have a flower bed or houseplants, it's also wise to just removed it if you don't want it to get chewed or dug up.

Introducing Your Siberian Husky to Your Other Pets

Siberian husky can get along with other dog breeds especially with their own kind. If you're keeping other dog breeds, give them time to sniff around with one another once your new pet arrives. Make sure to monitor their interaction and supervise them at least for the first few weeks. Usually Siberian huskies don't show aggression toward other dog breeds but your other dogs can have the potential to resent a newcomer so just be patient, you might see some mini confrontations in the onset which is why it's important that you supervise them at first until they get used to your new dog.

Make sure to not let all your dogs eat their food in the same place at least until you see them finally getting along. This can minimize territoriality and jealousy. Ensure that they have their own cage whenever you leave the house.

If you have a cat or other small furry creatures as well as reptiles and fishes, you might want to keep them out of sight because no amount of introduction and commands will stop your Siberian husky from preying on these household pets. However, there are many instances of tolerance on part of the Siberian husky but why risk it? Siberian huskies are gentle and can be trained but sometimes they can't fight their innate hunting instinct that could lead them to stalk small animals.

Don'ts to Keep in Mind

- Don't let your pet overtake you as the alpha. If you lose your lead and dominance, you'll end up having a disobedient Siberian husky. It's important that you establish yourself as the leader and be firm with your commands to let him know who's the "boss" is.

- Don't tolerate your pet's unwanted behavior. What you want to do is to correct it as early as possible so that it'll be easier for you to discipline him/ her in the future.

- Don't let your pet out in the yard or outside the house unleashed and unsupervised. Before you let them play outside, make sure that your gates are locked, the fences are strong, and that there are no holes through which they'll be able to slip out.

- Don't let him loose especially if you're walking him out. Siberian huskies are natural runners, and if they run lose there's no chance that you can catch up on him (unless you're a runner yourself). Use a leash when you're walking out to prevent him getting distracted and chasing other pets.

- Don't let your kids walk alone with your husky outside because your Siberian husky can easily run off and get lost.

- Don't let this dog breed hang around toddlers or babies unsupervised. The Siberian husky wouldn't harm them but they can get knocked off in the process as these dogs can be quite playful.

- Don't leave your small pets with your Siberian husky. Monitor their interaction and always supervise them even if they already get along with one another.

Chapter Six: Feeding Your Siberian Husky

One of the best things about keeping a Siberian husky is that they are not picky when it comes to food, and to most people's surprise they are light eaters. This is probably because they were raised in conditions during the time of the Chukchi tribes wherein they were trained to carry loads and walk for long hours with light tummies. They eat a lot less than most dog breeds of their size such as the Alaskan Malamute, and Samoyed breed. It's actually quite surprising how little they consume food considering the amount of energy they possess. This chapter will provide you with a wealth of information about what to feed your dog, how much and how often as well as some FAQs for new keepers.

The Ideal Weight for Your Siberian Husky

For you to keep your new pet healthy you'll need to provide him with the right diet and also regulate the amount of food he/ she eats. Watching their weight is wise to ensure that they are not underweight or overweight as both cases can impact their overall health. The Siberian Husky sire (male dogs) should have an ideal weight of around 45 to 60 pounds. On the other hand, female dogs or dams should have an ideal weight of 35 to 50 pounds. You should see to it that your pet stays within his or her prescribed weight because obviously a thin or fat Siberian Husky is not a healthy one.

Overfeeding your pet can take a toll on its health in the long run. The right diet and adequate exercise will keep your pet lean, active, and strong against illnesses. Usually, the amount of food a Siberian Husky needs is determined by the activities that he or she is engaged in. A Siberian husky that is used for work, for racing or for show will definitely need a different kind of food and amount compared to Siberian huskies that are just household pets.

How to Determine a Healthy Diet

Every animal breed has its own set of nutritional needs. You can choose to feed your pet with commercial foods or homemade fresh foods as long as this diet is healthy and suitable for them. Here are some of the things you need to keep in mind when it comes to providing the right nutrition:

- Nutrient sources that are quite the same in their diet in the wild are great as this is familiar to them. If the food is quite familiar they won't have a hard time adjusting, and they can easily digest their food.

- The diet should have the right amount of protein, fatty acids, vitamins, carbohydrates, and minerals that will suit their specific needs.

Diet of the Siberian Husky in the Wild

This is what these dogs eat in the wild, you might want to use this as a basis of the kind of nutrients or ingredients that will be included in your pet's food whether commercial dog foods or fresh foods. The diet of a Siberian Husky would have to include a blend of fish and poultry to provide him the fats and proteins he needs:

- Salmon
- Fresh water fish
- Animals like otter and mink

Nutritional Needs for Your Siberian Husky

The carbs required per kilogram of your pet's body weight should be much lower compared to other dog breeds. Siberian huskies will need a higher intake of fatty acids and also a balance of the following minerals:

- Linolenic Acid
- Linoleic Acid
- Oleic Acid

When deciding what kind of diet you'll provide for your pet, it's ideal that you ask your breeder for any recommendations. Your breeder would inform you all about what diet the puppy is on at the moment and would recommend what you need to give him in the future, once your Siberian husky becomes an adult. In case of a puppy you would need to follow the same diet that he or she is used to at least until they are old enough to try something totally new. Any sudden changes in diet would irritate his digestive system and could make your pet ill.

Ideal Ingredients for Your Siberian Husky Diet:

- Chicken meal (should be from a human – grade processing plant)
- Eggs (can be both raw and cooked since it has complete protein content and also has Vitamin A, Vitamin B, Vitamin E, Vitamin K, sulfur, biotin and amino acids)
- Fishmeal (should contain Omega – 3 Fatty Acids as this can improve your pet's coat and skin)
- Pork and red meats
- Poultry
- Uncooked bones (not too big or hard as it could chip your pet's teeth)
- Carrots, Spinach, Celery, Alfalfa leaf, grapes, apples, and garlic (these foods provide strong antioxidants for your pet
- Cottage cheese, whole milk or lactose reduced milk (avoid skim milk).
- Don't include corn, wheat and other products with artificial flavoring and colors

Some Reminders:

- As much as possible avoid feeding your Siberian husky with table scraps. Feeding them table scraps can give your pet diarrhea or become unhealthy. Ensure to feed him varied meals so as not to be disinterested in the same diet. Try feeding a mix of fresh food, canned food, and also dry food as long as you watch what they eat they're going to be fine.

- Avoid feeding him with foods like beef, soy, yellow corn, avocado, beet, horsemeat, cereals, onion, and chocolate.

Ideal Food Schedule for Siberian Huskies

For Young Pups

- It's important that you follow the meal routine set by your breeder (which can be around 3 to 4 times a day).

- Avoid overfeeding and giving him table craps because their stomachs at this age is not yet strong enough and could most likely upset his stomach.

3 to 4 months: 2 meals per day (same food)

7 to 9 months: 1 meal a day

8 to 10 months onwards: 1 meal a day (you can gradually start switching to adult dog foods)

18 months onwards: At this point, your Siberian husky is already considered as a mature adult dog which means that the meal you'll provide depends on how much exercise or activity your pet gets or needs. Occasional treats such a dog biscuit in the morning or cottage cheese with honey when he is on once a day feeding is all right.

Usually, a working Siberian husky would need a diet and amount that can increase his performance. This is the reason why it's very important to monitor their weight and make sure that they get adequate exercise.

Frequently Asked Questions

Should I feed my pet more if he/she looks underweight or thin?

As long as you're providing your pet with a healthy diet, and your meeting all the nutrients he/she needs at a certain age, it doesn't matter if your Siberian husky looks thin. They should in fact look sturdy and not fluffy or bloated. They should be active, capable of running fast, hiking, and walking without catching their breath too much. If ever you see him breathing heavily after running or walking, then it's best to consult your doctor. Other than that, you don't have anything to worry about. Never feed your pet more than the amount he/ she needs. Consult your breeder and veterinarian for advice on whether your Siberian Husky needs more food or maybe additional supplements and vitamins, but do not feed him or her additional food because you feel that they look "thin" or unhealthy.

When's the right time to switch from puppy food to adult dog food?

Most keepers switch foods once their pups hit 9 months. It's still best to consult your breeder or vet so you can ensure what age is appropriate to change their diet. Some people introduce adult food earlier than 9 months, while some do it a little over 10 months which is why it's best to ask your vet/ breeder about it as they already have knowledge and experience regarding this matter.

How to Determine if You Are Giving the Right Diet

- If the diet contains the right amount of proteins and fatty acids
- If you're feeding him healthy treats
- If your dog's coat and skin have no signs of dryness and itchiness. There should be no spots, flakes, and yeast infections in its ear

- If your pet don't have a liver, thyroid or kidney problem
- If your pet don't experience diarrhea
- If your pet is active, energetic, and can run or walk easily without being tired
- If your pet is alert and smart to follow simple commands
- If he/she doesn't look bloated or fat, and the weight is appropriate for his/her age.

Chapter Seven: Showing Your Siberian Husky

Siberian huskies have been around for almost 3000 years but it didn't become known until the breed reached Alaska. After establishing its claim as a pure bred dog, the American Kennel Club or AKC officially recognized the Siberian Husky breed and rewarded it with an official seal of approval. The first AKC registered Siberian Husky is called Fairbanks Princess Chena. If a dog breed became part of the AKC, it means that there's an official breed standard that breeders of Siberian Huskies should follow in order to maintain the purity and status of the breed. This is where showing your dog comes in.

This chapter will provide you with a wealth of information about the showing standards for your Siberian huskies. There are many dog showing competitions being held at different places, and the way to win is to ensure that your Siberian Husky's physical and behavioral characteristic comes close to the standard or is aligned with the dog standard of the breed. This is how judges can determine that your pet is "show quality," as it reached the highest standard of breeding.

Siberian Husky Official Breed Standard

Below is the official breed standard guideline as laid out by the American Kennel Club (AKC). Do take note that if you live in other countries, there'll most likely be a difference when it comes to the breed standards as it depends on the governing dog organization of the country where you live in.

General Physical Description

- The ideal Siberian Husky must showcase his heritage, through his appearance. It should be able to function with his harness on and pull a light load at a good enough speed over great distances just like how it was raised in Chukchi tribe.

- The husky should be quick, agile, effortless, and graceful on his feet and also have a moderately compact body with the right amount of fur.

- The dog should also show elegant and graceful actions and gait

- The husky should be alert, have an erect ears and a brush tail

- The husky's overall appearance should showcase a balance of strength, speed, and stamina. He should also convey power.

- According to the AKC, male huskies should look masculine without being coarse, and female huskies should look feminine without looking weak.

- Both males and females should show a firm and well – developed body structure with no excess weight. In short, your pet should be lean.

- The ideal height for male huskies is between 21 and 23 ½ inches at the withers, and not taller than that. On the other hand, females should be around 20 to 22 inches.

- The ideal weight should be proportionate to its height. For male huskies, it should be between 45 and 60 pounds while for female huskies it should be between 35 and 50 pounds. In the show ring, Siberian Huskies with too much of bone showing or too much weight can be penalized.

Head

- **Skull:** The skull should be medium in size since Siberian huskies are medium – sized dogs. Ideally, it should be quite rounded on the top, and shouldn't look clumsy or too heavy on the dog's body. It should be proportionate, and should not appear sharply chiseled.

- **Expression:** Despite of the wolfish looks, the husky should look friendly, keen, and also mischievous.

- **Eyes:** The eyes can be color brown or blue or both (1 blue – colored eye; 1 brown - colored eye). Parti – colored eyes is allowed as well. It should be almond in shape and must not be too obliquely set between the eyes.

- **Ears:** The ears should be thick, medium in size, and triangular in shape. It should be erect, and set higher up in their head with the tips pointing straight up. It should also have just enough fur, and shouldn't be set apart too wide.

- **Muzzle:** Should be medium in length, width, and taper off to its nose. It shouldn't be pointed or square.

- **Nose:** The nose color should be according to their coat color. Gray, tan or black Siberian Huskies have black noses while copper dogs have liver - colored noses, and a pure white Siberian Husky has a flesh - colored nose.

- **Lips and Teeth:** The lips should be well – pigmented and close fitting. The teeth should come close to a scissors bite.

Neck, Topline and Body

- **Neck:** The neck should be proud and erect when standing up. It should also be medium in length, and appropriate arched.

- **Chest:** The chest should be deep and strong but not broad. The ribs should also be well – sprung and flat at its side.

- **Back body:** It should be straight and strong. It should medium in length, and not slack. The loin should be lean and narrow than the rib cage. A sloping or slack topline is a fault.

- **Tail:** The tail should just be below the topline's level. If should also be a fox – brush shape. Must have enough fur in it. The tail should bend elegantly when the dog is alert to form a sickle curve. It shouldn't be curl to the side or lie flat on its back.

Forequarters and Hindquarters (Front/ Back Legs and Feet)

- **Forelegs:** The front legs should be moderately spaced, parallel and straight. The elbows should be close to the body and must not turn either in or out. The bones should look sturdy but not heavy. It is acceptable to remove the dewclaws on the forelegs.

- **Hind Legs:** The back legs should look powerful and strong. It should also be adequately spaced and parallel. The upper thighs should have strong muscles and the stifles or the dog's knee should be well bent. The dewclaws of the hind legs should be removed.

- **Feet:** It should be oval in shape. Must not be too long. The paws should be medium in size, and the pads should be thick and hard. There should be a good amount of fur, and the toes shouldn't be large or soft.

Coat

- Siberian huskies should have a double coat that is not long.

- The hair should be medium length with a well - furred look.

- The undercoat of the Siberian Husky should be soft and thick and long enough to prop up the outer coat.

- The guard hairs of the outer coat should be straight and kind of smooth.

- The hair should not stand straight up or be harsh.

- If your Siberian husky has a very long coat that is rough or too shaggy, it will be considered as faults.

Color

- Black to pure white colors is acceptable
- Variety of markings or masks in its head is also acceptable

Gait

- The breed should have a graceful way of walking
- It should be smooth, elegant, and effortless
- The breed should be light and quick on his feet
- The forequarters and hindquarters should show power, balance, and steadiness while walking or trotting off.
- Choppy walk or crossing is regarded as faults

Temperament

- The Siberian Husky should come off as friendly and gentle, but also attentive and outgoing.

- The breed should not have the suspicious and possessive alertness of a watchdog and should be good with strangers and other dogs.

- A Siberian Husky can be sociable, but he shouldn't be the over eager or obsess type.

- The dog breed should have a mature and reserved attitude.

- The temperament of the Siberian Husky should reflect his intelligence and prove him as a loyal companion dog as well as an eager and efficient working dog.

Chapter Eight: Grooming Your Siberian Huskies

The Siberian husky is regal looking pets with smooth coat and variety of markings. The best part is that you don't need to put in a lot of work to make your Siberian husky look really good. They are low maintenance pets that are very easy to groom and clean up. In fact, some keepers might even tell you that this dog breed knows how to clean themselves up just like cats. They also don't have that "dog odor" compared to other dog breeds. And since these dogs are so hygienic, they hardly need more than a bath in a year! This chapter will teach you things other grooming stuff that Siberian huskies may need help on that includes shedding, clipping of nails, cleaning its ears and the likes.

Shedding

Perhaps the main downside regarding keeping a Siberian husky is that they shed – A LOT. You can literally pile up all those furs on the ground and form a fluff mountain out of it, that's how much they shed. Siberian Huskies have a double coat, which is why during shedding season; they actually blow out their entire undercoat. Siberian Husky males shed once a year, while females shed twice a year around spring time and during fall. Shedding can last for around 3 weeks to a month.

Don't be surprised if your dog has bald patches in its body during this period, and if all your furniture is full of clumps of hair! However, all this is essential to keep your pet insulated and also encourage the growth of a new and smoother coat. Once the shedding period comes to an end, you'll find that your pet will not shed as much until the next shedding period. By then, he'll be very easy to care for because all you have to do is give him the right diet to maintain good skin and coat, brush your pet regularly, trim his nails every now and then, check his teeth, and give him a bath if need be.

Some newbie Siberian husky keepers such as yourself will ask this question: does the climate affect you're the husky's shedding? The answer is yes. If you live in a colder climate, you'll find that there will be seasons when your pet shed out its undercoat completely. If you live in a more humid climate, the shedding periods might be more diffused with your pet shedding all year round. However, if you live in a climate that has high humidity levels or gets very hot the shedding could be worse.

You have to understand that the double coat is what protects your pet from the varying degrees of seasons/ climate. The undercoat keeps them warm during the winter season. On the other hand, shedding the under coat during summers is their way to cool off.

Grooming Needs

You should keep in mind to not shave your pet's coat. Their coat protects them from the sun, rain, and snow. If you want your pet Siberian to have a nice undercoat, you can do that by feeding them with foods like fish that are rich with omega fatty acids. These types of food can help to improve your pet's skin, make their coat glossy, and can even reduce the shedding.

Grooming your dog is essential as it can help maintain its smooth skin, glossy coat, and also be free of mites and other irritants that could bring itchiness and illnesses to him.

Another importance of grooming is that it's a way for you to bond with your pet. It gets your dog used to your touch and makes him more open to human handling, which is why it's wise to start grooming your puppy as early as possible. Apart from that grooming can also be the time when you give your pet a thorough check up of his body. You can check for any sort of lumps, parasites, mites, cuts and prevent skin or ear problems.

Grooming Tools

Below are some of the basic things you need so that you can properly groom your Siberian husky.

- Shed blade
- Coat rake
- Curry brush (rubber)
- Wide – toothed metal comb
- Pin brush
- Dog – friendly shampoo and conditioner
- Towel
- Blow Dryer
- Nail Clippers
- Spray bottle (with water)

Steps in Bathing Your Siberian Husky

Step #1: Brush your Siberian Husky. Using the shed blade or coat rake, ensure to brush off all the loose undercoat, and make sure that there are no mats. If you put your pet under the water without brushing you will tangle up his hair even more.

Step #2: Provide a rubber mat in the bathtub. This is to prevent your dog from slipping off. Put your dog in the tub after brushing him and keep talking to him soothingly.

Step #3: Make sure that your dog's skin/ coat is wet with warm water. Since your dog's fur is quite dense, it would take around 15 to 20 minutes to wet him all over.

Step #4: Apply the shampoo and conditioner. Dilute the shampoo before you apply it all over his body. Make sure that the shampoo is dog – friendly, choose a whitening shampoo for light or white Siberian Huskies. Never use your own shampoo as this could be harmful for your pet. Use a rubber curry brush to rub your pet to stimulate your dog's body oils. You should opt to use a conditioner with sunscreen. A conditioner type would give the darker red dogs keep their color and prevent black dogs from developing a red tinge from the sun.

Step #5: Rinse him off. Make sure that there's no trace of shampoo left as it could irritate your pet and make him/ her itch.

Step #6: Dry him off using a towel and blow dryer. Dry him off and use a blow dryer to dry the water on his skin. Blow drying can also blow away the residue and loose fur in your pet's undercoat. Use the undercoat rake to brush him again.

Step #7: Brush him twice a week and bathe him again next year. Bathing your pet will depend on you of course, but you can opt to bathe them once or twice a year if you want. As mentioned earlier, your Siberian husky won't have any bad odor compared to most dog breeds as they always clean themselves up. If you bathe your Siberian Husky more than he needs it, you could be robbing his coat of some essential body oils that keeps his coat glossy.

Brushing Your Siberian Husky

When it comes to brushing your pet's coat, you'll find that you'll rake more than just brush as their coats are dense. The goal of brushing your dog regularly is to always get rid of the loose hair and keep the coat smooth and clean.

- Get rid of the clumps of hair. This is where you'll need the shed blade. After getting rid of the clumps of hair, you should brush your Siberian husky with a coat rake. You can start from the head and work towards the rest of its body.

- You can also add a few drops of conditioner in the water and spray it to your pet's coat. This will help control the static, loosen mats and also prevent hurting as you untangle some mats in your pet's coat.

- Once you got rid of the mats, the next thing to do is use the metal comb to comb the coat and flatten it out, then add some finishing touches by using a regular pin brush.

Regular Brushing

Make sure to brush the coat of your pet at least once or twice a week. You can use a wide – toothed comb to do regular brushing as its rounded off tip will not hurt your pet's body. Here are some things to keep in mind when brushing your dog:

- Use the comb to untangle the mats and knots if any and loosen the dead hair. Don't pull off the mats as this will hurt your pet

- Brush the undercoat and use a fine – toothed comb to also brush the fur under its skin, chin, tail, and ears.

- Take the brush and comb its coat forward over its head and shoulders.

- Remember to also comb out the hair in its legs and rear end

- You can also trim up some excess fur in its feet or toes to make him look neat. Never shave or trim the coat of your Siberian Husky.

Preventing Ticks and Fleas

Most household pets like dogs and cats are very prone in acquiring ticks and fleas in their coats. This is the reason why you need to groom up your pet and do a routine check on their coat to ensure that there are no ticks, fleas or mites living in their hair.

The way to remove these critters is to use forceps. Check out the tips below:

- When removing ticks or fleas, make sure you lift out the entire thing and not leave some parts of it behind.

- When you spot a tick, you can dab it over with some regular Vaseline and then pull it out. You might see that your Siberian husky's skin looks a bit red and irritated at the spot where the tick was clinging but that is normal.

- Wash of the area or dab on some antibacterial.

Trimming the Nails

It's a must that you regularly check your pet's nails, and get him accustomed to your handling in order to make them feel at ease whenever your clipping their nails. You need to trim your pet's nails at least twice or thrice a week using nail clippers suitable for your pet. Here are some tips on how you can trim the nails:

- Push back the skin and make sure you can see the part of the nail you want to clip.

- Watch out for the quick, which is the vein that runs down the center of the nail and can cause bleeding if cut. You just need to apply a quick stop and press it down to stop the bleeding.

- Make sure that the dewclaws are cut and trimmed to size, this is important if you're going to present your dog for showing.

Cleaning Your Siberian Husky's Ears

Should you need to clean out your pet's ears, you may ask the vet first to show you the correct way in doing it to avoid harming your pet. Whenever you're cleaning your pet's ear, make sure to check the hair around the ears and inside the ears too for any signs of ticks and mite infestations. Remove them and dab with antiseptic solution.

Dental Care for Your Siberian Husky

One of the most important things when it comes to grooming is to also check your dog's gums and teeth. You can ask your vet or your breeder to show you how you can properly and carefully brush your pet's teeth. Usually when you take your dog out for a check – up, your vet will clean your dog's teeth and scrape off the tartar. If you have a dental rake you can scrape off the tartar yourself, just be careful. Check out the tips below:

- To get your Siberian husky to allow you in brushing his teeth, what you can do is hold his face and slowly stick your finger in, and feel his gums. Your dog may of course resist it, but he'll eventually get used to it.

- Once your dog got accustomed to it, you can then add toothpaste to your finger and rub it along your dog's teeth.

- After brushing it, make sure to open his mouth and check if his teeth and gums look healthy. If you see any rotting teeth, make an appointment with the doctor as rotting teeth can be a sign of internal problem as well.

- Make sure that your dog does not have bad breath. If he does, this could be a sign that he/ she has some other problems or because of too much tartar buildup.

Chapter Nine: Common Ailments of Siberian Huskies

Siberian huskies are generally healthy dogs until they reach their senior age. There are some illnesses that you can expect to come up once they grow old. As a responsible keeper, it's important and essential for you to know about these problems as well as what to expect so that you'll know what to do in case your husky gets sick. It's also wise to consult your vet about common illnesses that could affect your pet or attend seminars and join dog clubs so that you'll be updated to certain health issues or vaccinations needed as well as geriatric care. This chapter will cover some of the most common ailments that your Siberian husky can experience in its lifetime. Knowledge about these diseases can make you prevent it or treat your dog as early as possible.

Arthritis

About 30% of dogs are affected by arthritis. The swelling of joints, stiffness, difficulty and pain when running or walking is quite evident among canine breeds including your Siberian husky. It's a debilitating disease that's sometimes known as Degenerative Join Disease. If your pet has it, simple everyday actions can be difficult and painful for your dog. Some symptoms of arthritis include the following:

- Reluctance to walk, climb stairs, jump or play
- Limp in one or all legs
- Signs of lagging
- Difficulty in getting up or sitting down
- Pain when touched
- Personality change or mood change

If you notice such signs, it's wise to consult your vet to get the right treatment. There are lots of pet keepers who have found that alternative therapy shows great results. You can opt for that as long as you get recommendations from your vet.

Hearing Problems

Another common ailment as your Siberian husky ages is loss of hearing. You may find that your pet dog does not respond to your call and cannot follow your commands unless you repeat them often not because they don't want to follow you but because they can't hear you loud and clear. Most canine breeds often lose hearing sensitivity as they age. It's wise to request your vet to conduct auditory tests as well as check for ear diseases or infections to ensure that your dog don't have other problems like parasite infestation. Some keepers communicate using hand signals and touch if they find out that their dog has a hearing problem. Ensure that your family members and friends never startle your pet or approach the dog from behind as they can get shock and harm you since they can't hear, and may not be aware of the things around them.

Obesity

Another prevalent health issue among Siberian huskies is obesity. Same with other dog breeds and even humans, aging can reduce activity, slow down ones metabolism, and use up fewer calories resulting to your dog gaining weight. A thinner dog or underweight dog, although still not healthy, is still healthier than an obese one. This is because obesity can cause other serious illnesses particularly heart problems, respiratory diseases, and organ problems. It can also affect your Siberian huskies joints and muscles. If you find that your dog is in a moderately good condition with the onset of age, you may just have to reduce its normal diet to an optimum amount to maintain its weight.

Frequent Urination

Most Siberian Huskies experience the need for frequent urination as they grow old. Just as you adjusted to the dog's needs when it was a puppy, it will once again need your assistance. You may need to take your pet out to eliminate 2 to 3 times at night. If in case the Siberian Husky experiences urine leak, it's highly recommended that you consult your vet as they will advise you on what to do. Make sure to spread a polythene sheet or washable pad over your dog's bed. If your dog wets its bed, be patient, and understand them. Don't shout or punish it especially if they are nearing their senior years. Make sure to wash the bedding frequently using solutions in order to reduce odors. Dry the bedding in the sun and as much as possible, always try and keep the bedding dry and clean to avoid further infections due to unsanitary environment.

Dental Disease

Another huge health issues for most dog breeds is dental disease. You need to regularly check your pet's teeth and gums to ensure that it is still healthy and to check for any infections, redness or sores. You can ask your vet about tips on how to care for your dog's dental hygiene. Your vet may recommend special creams and medications, or even a change in diet.

Most of the time oral infections are sometimes a sign of more grave internal problems, which is why your vet may recommend that you run essential tests to check for any other illnesses. Common symptoms of dental disorder include bad breath, inflamed gums, gingivitis, tartar build – up, and caries.

Vision

Another common problem of old age Siberian huskies is their vision. If you see cloudy eyes in your pet, you might want to go and have him check to the vet. As the eyes lose retinal cells and the retina becomes disorganized, the lenses of your pet's eyes also lose focus. Eventually loss of sight sets in.

The Siberian Husky will compensate for the loss of its vision through using their sense of smell and other instincts such as touch or hearing. If ever your pet does lose its sight, then you will need to help him by not changing or altering the positions of objects in your house. The environment must remain exactly to what the dog is familiar with. Otherwise, your Siberian husky may become confused and disoriented.

Constipation and Diarrhea

Diarrhea and constipation is common among aging Siberian huskies. Again, this is usually because of the lack of exercise, and the weakening of their digestive system. Your dog may not be able to digest its food properly as it ages which is why your vet may recommend methods to keep your Siberian husky as free as possible from these two problems. You'll most likely need to make subtle changes in your pet's diet. Sometimes the problem may not be because of old age but due to intestinal infections or even tumors. Consult your vet to ensure that your dog is in check.

Chest Diseases

Heart and lung problems are inescapable especially when your Siberian husky reached their senior years. They are very susceptible to it despite of all the measures you take beforehand. Routine check - ups at the vet will reveal any onset, and the vet will not just prescribe medications but also educate you on the precautions as well as care you need to do. Such precautions may include the following:

- Administer cautiously the medications prescribed by the vet to improve quality of life
- Limit the salt content in your dog's diet
- Monitor your dog's weight
- Limit your pet's activities. They are not allowed to do any strenuous activities like when they were still young.

Reproduction – Related Problems

If your pet hasn't been spayed or neutered before they reached 6 months, they can eventually develop health problems as they grow older. Usually, prostate diseases in male dogs, and uterine infections or breast cancers in female Siberian huskies are very common. Here are some tips to keep in mind especially if you're going to acquire a puppy, and to prevent such problems:

- You should get the dog spayed or neutered before its first birthday.

- If your pet is the breeding quality, consider spaying/neutering soon after it has had litters.

- The vet must examine any lump in the female breast tissue during routine check – ups.

- Blood in urine of male dogs must be reported to the vet for further diagnosis

Chapter Ten: Siberian Husky Checklist and Summary

You have gone through a lot when you have read this book, now, it is time for you to buy your puppy and apply these things in real life! You can search up for more information through other books or websites for further knowledge. This will enable you to become the best breeder with happy and healthy puppies. This last part will give you the overview of our beloved furry friend. Take note of these things as they might come handy someday.

Quick Checklist of Siberian Husky

Basic Information

- **Pedigree**: Siberian Husky
- **AKC Group**: Working dog group
- **Breed Size**: Medium – sized dog
- **Height:** average 51 to 60 cm. Male huskies are between 21 and 23 ½ inches at the withers; females should be around 20 to 22 inches.
- **Weight:** average of 35 to 60 lbs. Male dogs should have an ideal weight of around 45 to 60 pounds; female dogs should have an ideal weight of 35 to 50 pounds.
- **Coat Length**: short and double coated
- **Coat Texture**: soft, fluffy, dense, glossy,
- **Color**: Siberian huskies have double coats that are mostly colored black and white, copper red and white, or gray and white. Some huskies possess pure white or even brown, reddish and biscuit shading coats. These dogs also have very unique facial patterns or markings; have white feet and legs as well as tail tips that add to its wolfish look
- **Temperament**: docile, sociable, intelligent, active, energetic, playful, elegant, reserved
- **Strangers**: very friendly around strangers
- **Other Dogs**: both genders get along with other dogs
- **Other Pets**: not recommended if you have smaller pets

- o **Training**: needs firm but gentle leadership
- o **Exercise Needs**: needs lots of exercise
- o **Health Conditions**: generally healthy but susceptible to diseases such as obesity, eye and ear problems, heart diseases, lung infections, reproduction – related health issues, arthritis
- o **Lifespan**: average 11 to 15 years

Temperament and Behavior of Siberian Huskies

- Siberian huskies are still predators when it comes to other animals especially smaller breeds. Their killer instincts are awakened if they see pets like birds, cats, rabbits, guinea pigs, lizards, turtles, and the likes. It's not advisable that you left them alone with your other pets because their predator instincts can kicked in.

- The Friendly Dog: Siberian huskies are sweet and love to socialize with other people.

- The Loving Buddy: They're not the usual lap dogs but they are capable of a lot of love. They protect their owners like how parents protect their kids; they'll do what they can, not just for their keeper but their keeper's family.

- The Playful Pet: Siberian huskies are very playful and have a sense of humor. He loves playing with kids and toys. It's highly recommended that you provide him with his own toys too.

- The Smart Husky: Siberian huskies are highly intelligent creatures that don't need to get told what to do. They have that uncanny ability to know just what is needed from him.

- The Stubborn Attitude: You can circumvent this stubborn attitude by simply being the more matured and smart keeper that acts as the leader or the alpha dog. Once they know who is in charge, their stubborn attitude will not be a problem.

- The Energetic Animal: Since Siberian huskies are energetic and active pets, you can expect them to always have an alert mind, and lively attitude. They are quite optimistic and confident creatures.

Is this the Right Breed for You?

- If you are a first time dog keeper
- If you prefer to have a watchdog or guard dog to look over your property and kids

- If you are out of the house most of the time because of work
- If you don't have the time to supervise the dog
- If you are looking for a pet that always want to cuddle and show affection to you
- If you want a lap dog
- If you want to get a dog that will follow every order you give him or play catch with.
- If you want a dog breed that can go off without being leashed
- If you keep other smaller animals
- If you are allergic to dog fur as this breed sheds a lot
- If you like everything to be organized and neat especially in your garden
- If you don't like an active dog

The Siberian Husky is suited for you if:

- If you previously owned other dog breeds
- If you want a dog that will get along with the family
- If you want to have a dog that'll be gentle to your kids
- If you have a yard and garden that's secured and properly fenced
- If you like a low maintenance dog
- If you want a hygienic dog that's odor free
- If you prefer a mature and reserved dog breed

- If you can tolerate excessive shedding
- If you can commit to give time to walk him around and provide adequate amount of exercise
- If you are firm and patient especially when it comes to training
- If you're not going to leave him alone all the time and if you have enough time to interact with him.

Tips in Selecting the Right Siberian Husky Pup

- The pup should be active, alert, and sociable
- The pup shouldn't be afraid of other puppies or humans
- The pup should have no eyes and ears discharge and shouldn't be pot – bellied.
- The gums should be pink in color.
- The pup shouldn't resist whenever you hold them or aren't afraid of human interaction, this is a sign that they have been properly socialized.
- The pups should have the right weight for its age.
- The pup's coat should be free of fleas, dirt and bald patches
- They shouldn't have diarrhea or should have a clean bottom.

Tips in Selecting the Right Siberian Husky Adult

- The dog should already be house broken which means that he/she should know basic commands, and have already formed good behavior patterns.

- If you're acquiring a pet from rescue centers, it's wise to find out why they were abandoned in the first place.

- It's ideal to find out what the dog's habits is, its temperament, how he/ she respond to commands, daily routine and also its history.

- Check their overall health status

- The dog should be alert, has a pleasant disposition and quite mischievous

- The body is free of any discharge, patches, and the fur should be clean and well – groomed.

- The husky shouldn't be fat or bulky; it should be a moderate sized dog with a compact body.

- The husky should be balanced whenever he stands or moves

- The husky shouldn't have any mobility problems; he should be light on his feet if he walks

- The husky should show elegance, speed, and power

- The dog shouldn't be taller than 23 ½ inches for a male and no taller than 22 inches for females.

Things to do Before Bringing Your Pet Home

Task#1: Choose your dog's veterinarian.

Task#2: Learn, learn, learn!

Task#3: Buy everything your Siberian Husky needs

Task#4: Decide on where the potty spot will be located.

Task#5: Schedule feeding time.

Task#6: Puppy – proof your house.

Task#7: Tight security is a must.

Task#8: Remove any toxic objects.

Feeding Your Siberian Husky

- Nutrient sources that are quite the same in their diet in the wild are great as this is familiar to them. If the food is quite familiar they won't have a hard time adjusting, and they can easily digest their food.

- The diet should have the right amount of protein, fatty acids, vitamins, carbohydrates, and minerals that will suit their specific needs.

Ideal Ingredients for Your Siberian Husky Diet:

- Chicken meal (should be from a human – grade processing plant)
- Eggs (can be both raw and cooked since it has complete protein content and also has Vitamin A, Vitamin B, Vitamin E, Vitamin K, sulfur, biotin and amino acids)
- Fishmeal (should contain Omega – 3 Fatty Acids as this can improve your pet's coat and skin)
- Pork and red meats
- Poultry
- Uncooked bones (not too big or hard as it could chip your pet's teeth)

- Carrots, Spinach, Celery, Alfalfa leaf, grapes, apples, and garlic (these foods provide strong antioxidants for your pet
- Cottage cheese, whole milk or lactose reduced milk (avoid skim milk).
- Don't include corn, wheat and other products with artificial flavoring and colors

Some Reminders:

- As much as possible avoid feeding your Siberian husky with table scraps. Feeding them table scraps can give your pet diarrhea or become unhealthy. Ensure to feed him varied meals so as not to be disinterested in the same diet. Try feeding a mix of fresh food, canned food, and also dry food as long as you watch what they eat they're going to be fine.
- Avoid feeding him with foods like beef, soy, yellow corn, avocado, beet, horsemeat, cereals, onion, and chocolate.

General Physical Description

- The ideal Siberian Husky must showcase his heritage, through his appearance. It should be able to function with his harness on and pull a light load at a good enough speed over great distances just like how it was raised in Chukchi tribe.

- The husky should be quick, agile, effortless, and graceful on his feet and also have a moderately compact body with the right amount of fur.
- The dog should also show elegant and graceful actions and gait
- The husky should be alert, have an erect ears and a brush tail
- The husky's overall appearance should showcase a balance of strength, speed, and stamina. He should also convey power.
- According to the AKC, male huskies should look masculine without being coarse, and female huskies should look feminine without looking weak.
- Both males and females should show a firm and well – developed body structure with no excess weight. In short, your pet should be lean.
- The ideal height for male huskies is between 21 and 23 ½ inches at the withers, and not taller than that. On the other hand, females should be around 20 to 22 inches.
- The ideal weight should be proportionate to its height. For male huskies, it should be between 45 and 60 pounds while for female huskies it should be between 35 and 50 pounds. In the show ring, Siberian

Huskies with too much of bone showing or too much weight can be penalized.

Grooming Tools

- Shed blade
- Coat rake
- Curry brush (rubber)
- Wide – toothed metal comb
- Pin brush
- Dog – friendly shampoo and conditioner
- Towel
- Blow Dryer
- Nail Clippers
- Spray bottle (with water)

Common Ailments

- Arthritis
- Hearing Problems
- Obesity
- Frequent Urination
- Dental Disease
- Vision
- Constipation and Diarrhea
- Chest Diseases
  Reproduction – Related Problems

Glossary of Dog Terms

Abundism – Referring to a pup that has markings more prolific than is normal.

Acariasis – A type of mite infection.

ACF – Australian Pup Federation

Affix – A puptery name that follows the pup's registered name; puptery owner, not the breeder of the pup.

Agouti – A type of natural coloring pattern in which individual hairs have bands of light and dark coloring.

Ailurophile – A person who loves pups.

Albino – A type of genetic mutation which results in little to no pigmentation, in the eyes, skin, and coat.

Allbreed – Referring to a show that accepts all breeds or a judge who is qualified to judge all breeds.

Alley Pup – A non-pedigreed pup.

Alter – A desexed pup; a male pup that has been neutered or a female that has been spayed.

Amino Acid – The building blocks of protein; there are 22 types for pups, 11 of which can be synthesized and 11 which must come from the diet (see essential amino acid).

Anestrus – The period between estrus cycles in a female pup.

Any Other Variety (AOV) – A registered pup that doesn't conform to the breed standard.

ASH – American Shorthair, a breed of pup.

Back Cross – A type of breeding in which the offspring is mated back to the parent.

Balance – Referring to the pup's structure; proportional in accordance with the breed standard.

Barring – Describing the tabby's striped markings.

Base Color – The color of the coat.

Bicolor – A pup with patched color and white.

Blaze – A white coloring on the face, usually in the shape of an inverted V.

Bloodline – The pedigree of the pup.

Brindle – A type of coloring, a brownish or tawny coat with streaks of another color.

Castration – The surgical removal of a male pup's testicles.

Pup Show – An event where pups are shown and judged.

Puptery – A registered pup breeder; also, a place where pups may be boarded.

CFA – The Pup Fanciers Association.

Cobby – A compact body type.

Colony – A group of pups living wild outside.

Color Point – A type of coat pattern that is controlled by color point alleles; pigmentation on the tail, legs, face, and ears with an ivory or white coat.

Colostrum – The first milk produced by a lactating female; contains vital nutrients and antibodies.

Conformation – The degree to which a pedigreed pup adheres to the breed standard.

Cross Breed – The offspring produced by mating two distinct breeds.

Dam – The female parent.

Declawing – The surgical removal of the pup's claw and first toe joint.

Developed Breed – A breed that was developed through selective breeding and crossing with established breeds.

Down Hairs – The short, fine hairs closest to the body which keep the pup warm.

DSH – Domestic Shorthair.

Estrus – The reproductive cycle in female pups during which she becomes fertile and receptive to mating.

Fading Pup Syndrome – Pups that die within the first two weeks after birth; the cause is generally unknown.

Feral – A wild, untamed pup of domestic descent.

Gestation – Pregnancy; the period during which the fetuses develop in the female's uterus.

Guard Hairs – Coarse, outer hairs on the coat.

Harlequin – A type of coloring in which there are van markings of any color with the addition of small patches of the same color on the legs and body.

Inbreeding – The breeding of related pups within a closed group or breed.

Kibble – Another name for dry pup food.

Lilac – A type of coat color that is pale pinkish-gray.

Line – The pedigree of ancestors; family tree.

Litter – The name given to a group of pups born at the same time from a single female.

Mask – A type of coloring seen on the face in some breeds.

Matts – Knots or tangles in the pup's fur.

Mittens – White markings on the feet of a pup.

Moggie – Another name for a mixed breed pup.

Mutation – A change in the DNA of a cell.

Muzzle – The nose and jaws of an animal.

Natural Breed – A breed that developed without selective breeding or the assistance of humans.

Neutering – Desexing a male pup.

Open Show – A show in which spectators are allowed to view the judging.

Pads – The thick skin on the bottom of the feet.

Particolor – A type of coloration in which there are markings of two or more distinct colors.

Patched – A type of coloration in which there is any solid color, tabby, or tortoiseshell color plus white.

Pedigree – A purebred pup; the pup's papers showing its family history.

Pet Quality – A pup that is not deemed of high enough standard to be shown or bred.

Piebald – A pup with white patches of fur.

Points – Also color points; markings of contrasting color on the face, ears, legs, and tail.

Pricked – Referring to ears that sit upright.

Purebred – A pedigreed pup.

Queen – An intact female pup.

Roman Nose – A type of nose shape with a bump or arch.

Scruff – The loose skin on the back of a pup's neck.

Selective Breeding – A method of modifying or improving a breed by choosing pups with desirable traits.

Senior – A pup that is more than 5 but less than 7 years old.

Sire – The male parent of a pup.

Solid – Also self; a pup with a single coat color.

Spay – Desexing a female pup.

Stud – An intact male pup.

Tabby – A type of coat pattern consisting of a contrasting color over a ground color.

Tom Pup – An intact male pup.

Tortoiseshell – A type of coat pattern consisting of a mosaic of red or cream and another base color.

Tri-Color – A type of coat pattern consisting of three distinct colors in the coat.

Tuxedo – A black and white pup.

Unaltered – A pup that has not been desexed.

Index

M

N

O

P

S

T

Photo Credits

References

Feeding – MyHusky.com

http://www.myhusky.com.au/husky-guide/feeding/

Health Alert – 10 Health Problems of Your Siberian Huskies – SiberianHusky.com

https://siberianhusky.com/health-alert-10-health-problems-siberian-huskies/

How to Groom Your Husky – Snowdog,guru

https://www.snowdog.guru/groom-husky

Our Best Grooming Tips for Your Siberian Husky – Rover.com

https://www.rover.com/blog/best-grooming-tips-siberian-husky/

Siberian Husky – Dogtime.com

http://dogtime.com/dog-breeds/siberian-husky#/slide/1

Siberian Husky – Vetstreet.com

http://www.vetstreet.com/dogs/siberian-husky

Siberian Husky – DogBreedsList.info

http://www.dogbreedslist.info/all-dog-breeds/Siberian-Husky.html#.Wo4eOvnwa1s

Siberian Husky – AKC.org

http://www.akc.org/dog-breeds/siberian-husky/

Siberian Husky Feeding Guidelines - Petsworld.in

https://www.petsworld.in/blog/siberian-husky-feeding-tips.html

Siberian Husky Guide – AnimalPlanet.com

http://www.animalplanet.com/breed-selector/dog-breeds/working/siberian-husky.html

Siberian Husky - Temperament & Personality – Petwave.com

http://www.petwave.com/Dogs/Breeds/Siberian-Husky/Personality.aspx

Siberian Husky Temperament: What's Good About 'Em, What's Bad About 'Em - YourPureBredPuppy.com

http://www.yourpurebredpuppy.com/reviews/siberianhuskies.html

What is the Best Dog Food for Siberian Huskies? The Ultimate Siberian Husky Food Buyer's Guide – dogfood.guru

https://dogfood.guru/siberian-huskies/

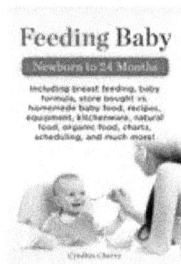

Feeding Baby
Cynthia Cherry
978-1941070000

Axolotl
Lolly Brown
978-0989658430

Dysautonomia, POTS
Syndrome
Frederick Earlstein
978-0989658485

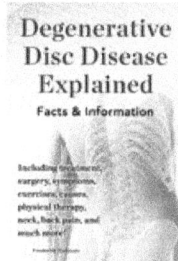

Degenerative Disc
Disease Explained
Frederick Earlstein
978-0989658485

Sinusitis, Hay Fever,
Allergic Rhinitis Explained
Frederick Earlstein
978-1941070024

Wicca
Riley Star
978-1941070130

Zombie Apocalypse
Rex Cutty
978-1941070154

Capybara
Lolly Brown
978-1941070062

Eels As Pets
Lolly Brown
978-1941070167

Scabies and Lice Explained
Frederick Earlstein
978-1941070017

Saltwater Fish As Pets
Lolly Brown
978-0989658461

Torticollis Explained
Frederick Earlstein
978-1941070055

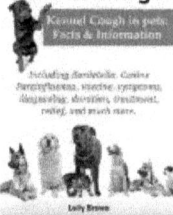

Kennel Cough
Lolly Brown
978-0989658409

Physiotherapist, Physical
Therapist
Christopher Wright
978-0989658492

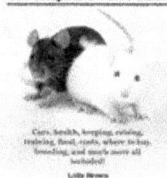

Rats, Mice, and Dormice
As Pets
Lolly Brown
978-1941070079

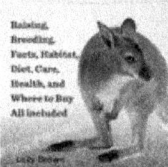

Wallaby and Wallaroo Care
Lolly Brown
978-1941070031

Bodybuilding Supplements
Explained
Jon Shelton
978-1941070239

Demonology
Riley Star
978-19401070314

Pigeon Racing
Lolly Brown
978-1941070307

Dwarf Hamster
Lolly Brown
978-1941070390

Cryptozoology
Rex Cutty
978-1941070406

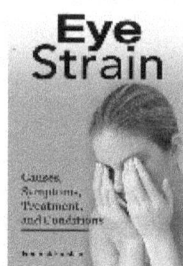

Eye Strain
Frederick Earlstein
978-1941070369

Inez The Miniature Elephant
Asher Ray
978-1941070353

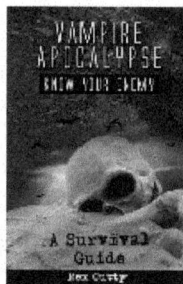

Vampire Apocalypse
Rex Cutty
978-1941070321

www.ingramcontent.com/pod-product-compliance
Lightning Source LLC
Chambersburg PA
CBHW052113090426
42741CB00009B/1797